Contents

The travel and tourism industry

Travel and tourism is one of the fastest growing industries in the world. People travel for business and to visit friends and family, and tourists visit and stay in other regions for a variety of reasons, such as adventure, relaxation and to see new places.

The travel and tourism industry provides tourists with the services and products they need to make their trip, such as transport to get them there and hotels and restaurants to stay and eat in.

Today many airline companies offer low-cost, scheduled air services, so many people can travel abroad for their holidays.

Tourism takes off

Tourism really took off in the latter half of the 20th century. Before that time, few people travelled far because transport costs were high, wages were low and time off for holidays was mostly unpaid. Those who could afford holidays travelled abroad by train or ship or within their own countries by car, coach or train. The rise in tourism after 1950 occurred mainly because of improvements in transport. The Boeing 707 jet plane was the first successful large, passenger plane and it ushered in the age of air travel for the masses. As planes got bigger and faster, they could carry more passengers, more quickly, so air fares reduced in price and tourist numbers exploded.

Development or DESTRUCTION?

Travel and Tourism

DATE DUE

T20331

First published in 2011 by Wayland
Copyright © 2011 Wayland

Wayland
338 Euston Road
London NW1 3BH

Wayland Australia
Level 17/207 Kent Street
Sydney NSW 2000

Editor: Nicola Edwards
Designer: Elaine Wilkinson
Proofreader: Hayley Fairhead
Map illustrator: Adrian Stuart

Spilsbury, Louise.
   Travel and Tourism. -- (Development or destruction?)
   1. Tourism--Juvenile literature. 2. Tourism--Case studies
   --Juvenile literature.
   I. Title II. Series
   338.4'791-dc22
ISBN 978 0 7502 6601 7

Picture acknowledgements:

The author and publisher would like to thank the following agencies for allowing these pictures to be reproduced: Cover: Shutterstock © Mike Liu; title page: Shutterstock; contents page: Shutterstock © KA Photography KEVM111; p6 (l) EyesWideOpen/Getty Images, (r) Shutterstock © Ipatov; p8 Alexander Joe/AFP/Getty Images; p10 (t) Shutterstock © skvoor; pp10-11 Shutterstock © Mike Liu; p12 (t) Shutterstock © Chad Zuber, (b) Shutterstock © Michael Vesia; p13 Shutterstock © holbox; p14 Shutterstock © Kate Connes; p16 (t) Shutterstock © skvoor; (m) Shutterstock © Rebecca Connolly; p17 (t) Shutterstock © Kenneth Sponsier, (b) iStock © Jim Parkin; p18 (t) Shutterstock © Nickolay Stanev, (b) © Stanislaw Tokarski / Shutterstock.com; p19 (t) Shutterstock © Nelson Hale, (b) iStock © Matt Kaminski; p20 Eric Paul Zamora/Fresno Bee/MCT via Getty Images; p23 (t) Shutterstock © Janne Hämäläinen, (b) © Arcticphoto/Alamy; p24 (t) Shutterstock © K. Thorsen, (b) Olivier Morin/AFP/Getty Images; p25 Jonathan Nackstrand/AFP/Getty Images; p26 (t) iStock © Arne Bramsen, (b) Gael Branchereau/AFP/Getty Images; p28 (t) Shutterstock © Atlaspix; (b) Leila Gorchev/AFP/Getty Images; p29 Chris Ratcliffe/Bloomberg via Getty Images; p30 Alex Mita/AFP/Getty Images; p31 © Jeff Morgan 09/Alamy; p32 (t) Laura Boushnak/AFP/Getty Images, (b) Shutterstock © Pawei Kazmierczak; p34 (t) Shutterstock © Roger De Marfa, (b) Shutterstock © KA Photography KEVM111; p36 (t) Shutterstock © skvoor; (b) Shutterstock © Rick Wylie; p37 © John Warburton-Lee Photography/Alamy; p38 © Paul Miles/Alamy; p40 Shutterstock © Karin Hildebrand Lau; p41 © Travelscape Images/Alamy; p42 Shutterstock © Evgeny Prokofyev; p43 © Victor Paul Borg/Alamy

Printed in China

Wayland is a division of Hachette Children's Books,
an Hachette UK company.
www.hachette.co.uk

Chapter 1

Types of tourism

The advent of package holidays, which are cheaper because tour operators take a big group of tourists on the same flights to the same hotels, led to mass tourism. Beach holidays at seaside resorts in the Mediterranean, North Africa and the Caribbean were the focus of mass tourism in the 1960s and 1970s.

After the 1980s, other technologies encouraged further growth in the industry. People wanted to visit interesting and exotic places they saw on the TV and then began to use the Internet to research and book their own holidays. Since the 1990s, the range of holiday types and destinations has increased and so has the number of tourists taking them.

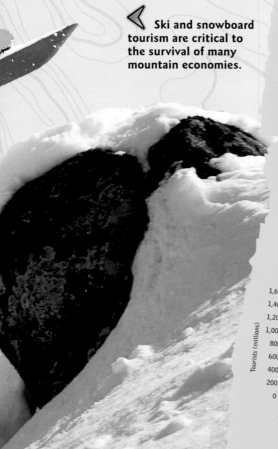

◁ **Ski and snowboard tourism are critical to the survival of many mountain economies.**

International tourists

International tourists are those who travel to foreign countries for a holiday. In 1950 there were only 25 million international tourists. As this graph shows, that number had reached over 1 billion by 2010 and is expected to reach 1.6 billion by 2020. The graph also shows how tourist destinations are changing. For a long time Europe dominated the industry, but as long-haul flights have become cheaper and less economically developed countries (LEDCs) have become more prosperous, travel patterns are changing. By 2020 the busiest destinations will be Europe (717 million tourists), East Asia and the Pacific (397 million) and the Americas (282 million), followed by Africa, the Middle East and South Asia.

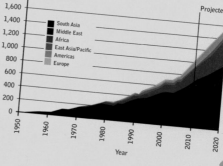

A global industry

Global tourism is one manifestation of globalisation. This means that tourist holidays impact on other people and places far away. Tourism can help people to learn to respect foreign cultures and above all can contribute to international cooperation and peace. It can stimulate economic development, because it has a high multiplier effect on economies. It creates many jobs, not only in hotels and restaurants, but also in other industries, such as theme parks. Revenue from tourism represents one of the main income sources for many LEDCs.

Development fact

Tourism provides 6 to 7 per cent of the world's jobs and millions more indirectly. The World Trade Organization (WTO) estimates that tourism accounts for 8 per cent of the global Gross National Product (GNP).

▽ South Africa's first high-speed train, the Gautrain, opened in time for the 2010 World Cup, linking Tambo International Airport with Johannesburg, the country's largest city. Infrastructure like this, built mainly for tourists, benefits local people too.

A destructive industry?

Some impacts of the tourist industry are destructive. Most international tourism is controlled by multinational companies based in more-developed countries (MEDCs), such as hotel chains with hotels in different destinations, so profits from a holiday in an LEDC end up back in MEDCs. Problems can occur if a country relies too heavily on the tourist industry, for example in beach resorts where there are high rates of unemployment during winter. Tourism also causes environmental problems, such as air pollution from vehicle emissions, habitat destruction when land is cleared for hotels, and overuse of natural resources such as water.

Destruction fact

Around 1.5 million residents of Beijing were displaced or evicted from their homes to make way for construction projects for the tourist-generating Olympic Games in China in 2008.

Pros and cons of tourism

There is already a wide choice of holidays, and every year new or expanded tourist markets and destinations appear. For example, in 2010 remote forest-covered valleys in Bhutan (where people claim to have seen yetis!) were newly opened to foreigners. What can Bhutan and others learn from the way tourism has affected people, wildlife and environments in other places?

Through the case studies in this book, located on the map below, we'll explore whether destruction is always an inevitable consequence of tourism or whether it can be used to aid development in countries, without negative impacts on people and the natural environment.

 Does tourism create development or destruction?

The challenge for national parks like Yosemite is how to attract tourists without destroying the natural world that tourist revenue pays to protect. (pages 16-21)

When tourists visit the Sami people of Sápmi (Lapland) are they helping to preserve that unique culture or helping to destroy it? (pages 22-27)

Find out about the environmental destruction caused by the Cancun beach resort in Mexico and what is being done to halt it. (pages 10-15)

Are package holidays to Ayia Napa in Cyprus using up water resources there and if so, what can be done about it? (pages 28-33)

How can safari companies in Kenya balance the demands of local people and tourists with the protection of wildlife? (pages 34-39)

MEXICO

Cancun City

Lagoon

Cancun
International
Airport

Caribbean Sea

Cancun is a purpose-built resort on a strip of land shaped like a number 7. It is linked by a causeway to Cancun City.

Tourists come to the island of Cancun on Mexico's Caribbean coast, for the white sandy beaches, palm groves, coral reefs and the region's warm, tropical climate.

Creating Cancun

Up until the 1960s, Cancun Island was a series of narrow sand dunes with just 12 families working in fishing and on a coconut plantation. At that time, the Mexican economy was struggling and Acapulco and Mexico City were the country's only international tourist destinations. So to compete with successful tourism destinations in the Caribbean Basin, in 1970 the Mexican government started to turn Cancun Island into a resort. The plan was for a tourist zone, served by an airport 11 kilometres away and a new city, Cancun City, to house people working at the resort.

Development fact

Cancun is the biggest money-earner of all of Mexico's tourist destinations, bringing in about a quarter of Mexico's total tourism income.

Chapter 2

By 1974 four hotels had also been built and after that private businesses started buying up land and building hotels and other commercial enterprises there. Workers dug wells for water, lay sewage pipes and electricity cables, and brought in huge amounts of soil to widen the island. They built a road to the airport that opened in 1974 and created a golf course.

Boom and benefits

Initially only the seaward side of Cancun was developed, as a luxury beach resort. From the 1980s more people arrived on package holidays, demanding more facilities and activities, such as water sports. More shops, restaurants, nightclubs and other commercial developments crowded onto the coast and on the lagoon side of Cancun and eventually in the city of Cancun too. The Cancun resort brought wealth and infrastructure to a region that previously had no prospect of urban development. In an area where there had been only agriculture and fishing, there was an increase in the number of industries, such as local services and construction.

▽ **Cancun is Mexico's largest tourism destination, attracting more international visitors per year than the capital, Mexico City.**

Growth of a resort

This graph shows how rapidly Cancun developed from a virtually uninhabited island in the 1970s to a resort visited by around 3 million tourists every year. By attracting people from other parts of the country the population increased to over 670,000 permanent residents by 2010.

The leap in visitors after the late 1980s coincides with the advent of package holidays to the region and lower air fares. Tourist numbers dropped slightly from 2001 to 2005 due in part to the 9/11 tragedy in the USA in 2001 and because a hurricane in 2005 put some hotels temporarily out of action.

Mangrove destruction

To build Cancun, 372,000 sq km (143, 630 sq miles) of mangrove forests were destroyed and the land drained. Mangroves protect coasts by lessening the impacts of sudden storms and they are important to fishing and timber industries. Mangrove wood can be harvested for timber and charcoal and many fish caught in tropical regions reproduce or shelter in mangroves or depend on food chains linked to mangroves. Almost 80 per cent of global fish catches are dependent on mangroves.

Mangroves grow in or near salt water along sheltered coastlines and estuaries.

Environmental impacts of mangrove loss

Loss of habitat also means loss of wildlife. The live and decaying leaves and roots of mangrove trees fed plankton, algae, shellfish, fish, crabs and shrimp and they were also home to many birds and mammals. The loss of the forests, and the fact that hotels were built too close to the sea, also resulted in coastal erosion. The intertwining roots of mangrove trees had held the sand together. Without them the beaches in front of the hotels are being washed away. The erosion has been worsened by hurricanes and by the fact that the sea level is rising by about 2.2 millimetres a year, possibly due to climate change.

Destruction fact

Mangroves are being lost three to four times faster than land-based forests. According to the United Nations, one fifth of all of the world's mangroves have been lost since 1980.

Beach erosion sometimes exposes rocks on beaches in Cancun.

ON THE SCENE

'Mangroves covered all the coastal area (of Cancun). They have just been paved over. This is the star example of how not to build a mass tourism mecca. It is an ecological mistake that should never have happened.'

Barbara Bramble, adviser to the National Wildlife Federation, Washington DC, USA

Reefs and mangroves

Another major impact of the loss of mangroves and the rise in tourism is the destruction of coral reefs off Cancun – around 70 per cent are in poor or critical condition. With fewer mangroves for fish to breed in, there are fewer fish. With fewer fish to eat some of the seaweed that grows on corals, reefs decline as corals are replaced by seaweed. Mangroves also absorb the run-off of fertilizers, pesticides and other pollutants from land, keeping coastal waters clean. This protects coral reefs from being smothered by sediment and from eutrophication, whereby nutrients in the water promote the growth of algae that smother corals.

Coral in crisis

There are other causes of coral decay. Reefs have been affected by overfishing and divers damage reefs if they touch, swim close to or take pieces of the corals. Corals are also affected by climate change. They are sensitive to temperature changes and many die as oceans get warmer.

Coral reefs are one of the most diverse habitats in the world, providing food and shelter for a wide range of marine life. They also protect coasts by absorbing some of the impact of storm waves.

Managing mangroves

Mexico is reducing mangrove destruction, partly because these trees help slow climate change. As they photosynthesize, they absorb carbon from the air and store it in their roots. In fact mangroves absorb up to 50 times more carbon than the same area of tropical forest. Another reason to protect mangroves is that when destroyed they release carbon. In 2010 a Cancun hotel exploded, killing five tourists. One possible cause was the build up of carbon gases from rotting mangroves buried under the hotel.

Innovations
Conserving corals

An innovative new way of conserving corals has been developed. In 2009, over 400 life-size sculptures of real people were anchored to an area of barren sea bed off Cancun. The sculptures are made from a special kind of cement that encourages coral growth. It is intended that they will attract divers away from the natural reef.

◁ **The Underwater Sculpture Museum, Cancun Marine Park.**

Caring for coasts

In 2010 sand was dredged from the bottom of the Caribbean Sea and used to rebuild Cancun beaches. The problem is that the beaches may wash away again. Also, removing huge amounts of sand like this affects ocean floor ecosystems. Environmentalists suggest planting more vegetation in areas between hotels and beaches so that the roots will help to stabilize the impacts of erosion along the coast.

EXPLORE FURTHER

Find out how the Great Barrier Reef in Australia, which attracts 2.5 million tourists a year, is being protected.

Cancun's future

Cancun faces new problems in the future. The Mexican government created Cancun from scratch to bring prosperity to the region, but much tourism revenue is going to foreign corporations and not to local communities. Many tourism workers earn low wages and live in poor-quality housing in Cancun City. Faced with a lack of money, criminal gangs dealing in drugs have formed. Two of the city's mayors are facing criminal charges, accused of having worked with them. Officials fear that stories of drug-related violence will put tourists off, which is particularly bad news as tourism is the only industry in Mexico that is generating new jobs.

Development or Destruction?

Development

* Cancun developed from a virtually deserted island to Mexico's largest tourist destination.
* The Cancun resort brought wealth and infrastructure and new industries to an undeveloped region.
* Cancun brings in about a quarter of Mexico's total tourism income.

Destruction

* To build Cancun, 372,000 sq km (143,630 sq miles) of mangrove forests were destroyed.
* Loss of mangroves and building hotels close to the sea caused coastal erosion and damaged coral reefs.
* Many tourism workers earn low wages and live in poor-quality housing.

Yosemite National Park, USA

National parks are areas of land protected because of their beautiful countryside, wildlife or cultural heritage. National park designated areas have staff to enforce laws that ensure that visitors and residents use the land without destroying it.

Balancing the need for park developments with restrictions to protect land and wildlife can be tricky. Yosemite, a 3000-sq-km (1, 158-sq-mile) park in the Sierra Nevada valley, USA, is a case in point.

State of California

Yosemite National Park

San Francisco

Sequoia and Kings Canyon National Parks

Los Angeles

San Diego

Early days

When Europeans arrived in the Yosemite area in the mid-1800s, they found the Ahwahneechee tribe, who had lived there for generations. These Native Americans were forced out of the area by white gold miners and settlers, and news soon spread about the beauty of the region's waterfalls, deep valleys, wide meadows, giant sequoia trees and areas of wilderness. The initial developments began immediately and within a few years lodges opened for the first tourists, who arrived by horse or stagecoach. As more businesspeople moved in to exploit more of the land, conservationists appealed for it to be protected.

ON THE SCENE

'We keep hearing it said that we are 'loving our parks to death,' but what we really need to know and help others know is how to love our parks.'

Superintendent David A. Mihalic, Yosemite National Park

Yosemite National Park is famous for its giant sequoia trees.

Chapter 3

In 1864 President Abraham Lincoln signed a bill granting Yosemite Valley and the Mariposa Grove of Big Trees to the State of California. The National Park was created in 1890 and was protected by the US cavalry until the National Park Service was established in 1916.

Attracting tourists

Tourism in Yosemite National Park boomed during the 20th century and today around 4 million people visit every year, 90 per cent of which are domestic tourists. Funds raised by the fees and permits charged by the Park are used to maintain and improve it. Visitors, companies and supporters also donate over US$1 million a year to Yosemite charitable funds, which are used for things like habitat restoration and trail maintenance. The Park also receives revenue from hotels and other commercial enterprises that do business within it.

People come to Yosemite for the views and the wildlife and to enjoy a wide range of visitor attractions, including shops, restaurants, a golf course, swimming pools, tennis courts and a ski resort.

Vital statistics: Yosemite

Number of buildings: 1237
Number of campsites: 1504, with a maximum of 9,372 campers
Number of bridges: 127
Number of road tunnels: 4
Length of hiking trails: 1287 km (800 miles)
Length of roads: 454 km (282 miles)

Driving development

Cars were legally admitted to Yosemite in 1913, when just 127 entered. In 2008, 423,689 vehicles drove into the park through just one of its four major entrances. Motor traffic helped the park to become one of the most popular tourist destinations in America, but it is also one of its major problems.

As the number of cars entering the Park increased, more car parks and roads had to be built, which has caused habitat loss. Traffic also causes air pollution, especially when cars sit in traffic jams during busy summer months. Yosemite Valley is known as a honeypot site because more than 90 per cent of tourists visit only this huge canyon. At times car exhaust emissions containing nitrogen oxides, particles, carbon monoxide and hydrocarbons can accumulate here and have a damaging impact on the health of plants and animals.

Vital statistics:

Cars prices and visitor numbers

Year	Cost of a Model 'T' Ford	Yosemite visitors
1908	US$850*	8,850
1912	US$590	10,884
1916	US$360	33,390
1922	US$300	100,506

*nearly US$17,000 in today's dollars

ON THE SCENE

'There's not a whole lot of parking, so people just park wherever sometimes and don't notice what they're doing to the nature in the Park.'

Mauricio Lopez-Rivera, Los Angeles resident and visitor to the Park

Parking and pollution

Another problem with vehicles is that in the busy summer months there are not enough car park spaces and frustrated drivers park illegally on roadside verges, where they damage the vegetation. This can cause soil erosion that makes soil infertile and reduces plant life in the park. Some visitors drive onto unpaved roads to find quiet spots, and the noise pollution from their vehicles disturbs wildlife, which is especially damaging at times when animals are mating, nesting or raising young.

More cars, more visitors

More cars mean more visitors and because most tourists stay in Yosemite Valley, their impact is concentrated here, in less than 1 per cent of the Park's total area! Most visitors follow park rules, but some stop their cars and walk across sensitive soil, trampling plants and killing seedlings. Areas of river banks close to camp sites have been eroded by visitors, destroying natural habitats and in dry summer months walkers that stray off designated trails can cause soil erosion. Careless campers make noise and leave litter, spill food, or allow plastic bags to blow away, disturbing or damaging wildlife.

Roads cut across wild land and in spite of signs asking visitors to drive slowly, cars sometimes hit wild animals.

Yosemite National Park is home to hundreds of American black bears and if visitors don't store food in lockers, bears steal it. Bears that often steal human food can become aggressive, and may have to be killed as a result.

Solutions: The Park plan

In 1980 a plan was laid out to restore meadows, remove some campsites and move others away from rivers, but little progress was made. Then in 1997 a severe flood damaged many roads and campsites and the US government approved US$175 million for rebuilding. However, in 2000, a lawsuit was filed by environmentalists who feared the money would be used for road-widening, new car parks and bigger buildings, bringing more cars and visitors to the park. A court order stopped the rebuilding and in 2009 Park authorities agreed to develop a new plan that includes a 'user capacity program', limiting the number of visitors. However, opponents say if access is limited, for example by increasing prices, far fewer people will be able to visit.

Tackling traffic

A plan to reduce vehicle traffic in Yosemite Valley is underway. Some old roads have been removed and one-way road traffic systems have been established to reduce traffic jams. Car parks along riverbanks have also been removed. Visitors are being encouraged to leave cars in a main parking area and travel by shuttle bus or tram.

Innovations: Hybrid Buses

In 2005 low-noise, fuel-efficient electric-hybrid shuttle buses began carrying tourists free of charge from car parks to the lodges and in 2009 new hybrid diesel tractor cabs started to power open air trams that tour Yosemite Valley. Hybrid vehicles combine fuel engines and electric motors to produce 80-90 per cent fewer emissions than pure fuel-burning vehicles.

◁ Hybrid shuttle buses at Yosemite National Park.

EXPLORE FURTHER

Find out more about national parks in the UK. Research where they are and how they differ from US national parks.

Lessons learned

Sequoia and Kings Canyon National Parks, also in California (see map on page 16), are jointly administered by park officials who learned from the problems in Yosemite. In Giant Forest in Sequoia National Park a restoration project has already demolished old buildings and moved roads and car parks to return the area to a more natural state and make it more attractive. Visitor numbers are already regulated. Even so, during a time of economic recession more domestic tourists are expected to visit these parks and the same challenge faces them all: how to welcome visitors without destroying a park's peace and beauty – the very things people come to see.

Development or Destruction?

Development

* Tourist revenue maintains Yosemite National Park, which protects its countryside and wildlife.
* Revenue from hotels and businesses within its boundaries also benefits the Park and creates employment.
* Tourists enjoy the Park's natural beauty and the visitor attractions provided for them.

Destruction

* Tourist car parks, roads and facilities cause habitat loss in the Park.
* Vehicles cause air and noise pollution and some speeding vehicles hit wildlife.
* Some visitors trample plants and erode soil and riverbanks.
* Campers can also cause litter and noise pollution.

Cultural tourism is when tourists visit a country to learn more about local people and their culture. It's a fast-growing sector of the tourism industry. In the last 20 years there has been a rise in the number of holidays to visit the Sami people.

This map shows the Sápmi area, where Sami people live. The area has no actual borders.

The Sami are the indigenous people of the region called Sápmi, sometimes known as Lapland, which covers the far north of Finland, Norway, Russia and Sweden.

The Sami people

The Sami people have their own language, culture, customs and traditions and their own parliament and flag. Traditionally the Sami people lived by fishing, hunting and reindeer herding. The reindeer-herding Sami lived in tents or turf huts and families migrated with their herds from the forests towards the Arctic coast where reindeers have their summer grazing and calving areas. Today only about one in ten adult Sami people are reindeer herders and they mostly travel by modern vehicles such as snowmobiles rather than on skis and dog sleds.

Many Sami people have settled in towns and work, for example in shops and offices, outside the traditional Sami occupations.

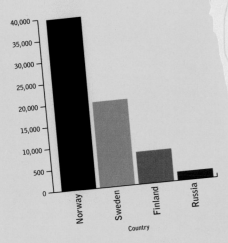

Sami people in Sápmi

This chart shows that of the 69,500 Sami people in the world, the majority live in Norway. Sweden has the second-largest population and Russia the lowest.

Problems with Sami tourism

An increasing number of tourists want to experience the Arctic wilderness where the Sami live and see the Sami people in their traditional colourful costumes with their reindeer. One problem is that driving groups of tourists out into the wilderness to see Sami people and the reindeer can harm the fragile Arctic environment.

Chapter 4

Motor vehicles cause noise pollution that disturbs wildlife, they can erode surfaces that have sparse plant or soil cover, and vehicle emissions can damage local ecosystems.

Selling Sami culture

Environmental damage is not a big issue yet, because most Sami tourism is centred in towns. The problem here is that tourism can alter and damage Sami culture by over-commercialisation. For example, when Sami people perform traditional 'joiks' (songs and chants) for crowds of tourists, some say this robs the joiks of their significance and reduces the Sami people to stereotypes. Traditional Sami handicrafts include reindeer horn knives and cups and beautifully embroidered clothes, but today many non-traditional Sami handicrafts are produced solely to appeal to tourists, such as imported dolls in plastic boxes wearing Sami costumes. Some people also say that mixing with other cultures and tourist influences means that Sami identity is becoming weaker and less distinct.

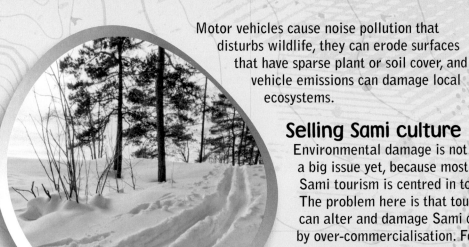

▲ Vehicles make tracks in the pristine Arctic landscape.

▽ These Sami women are selling handicrafts at the Kautokeino Easter Festival at Finnmark, North Norway.

70; STOR

60; LIT

Santa's helpers?

The Santa Claus Tourist Centre in Rovaniemi, Finland is a centre of international Christmas tourism. This popular destination contains many attractions, from ski slopes and ice sculptures to shops, and in the Santa Claus Village theme park tourists can meet Santa and his elves, who are dressed in traditional Sami-style clothing, or take sleigh rides pulled by reindeer who are then kept in garages or sheds in the town.

By making the connection between the Sami people and Santa's helpers, some Finnish businesses have opened up a new way to make money from the Sami culture. Non-Sami employees dress in fake Sami costumes in Rovaniemi and elsewhere, and sell a wide variety of fake Sami clothing, handicrafts and dolls. This has caused anger among many Sami people and in 2008 there was a protest in Rovaniemi by young Samis and politicians from all four Sami nations. Protesters say some tourist companies misrepresent the Sami culture by making it part of the Santa Claus tourist industry and that the Sami products they sell are not even made by Sami people. Many Sami people feel that this is an insulting display of cultural exploitation.

A reindeer decorated for the Christmas tourist season.

ON THE SCENE

'If tourist companies are going to present Sami culture, they have to present something that is real.'

Lars Miguel Utsi from the Saminuorra Sami youth organisation

A man wearing a traditional Sami costume leads a reindeer pulling a sleigh filled with children through Rovaniemi during the busy Christmas holiday season.

Promoting Sami culture

The Sami people of Norway and Sweden control their own tourist industries and this has brought many benefits, including job opportunities, higher incomes and the spread of Sami culture. Sápmi is a large area with limited infrastructure so there are few job options. Competition from larger companies, for example in Finland where anyone can herd reindeer, means that the prices Sami herders in Norway and Sweden get for reindeer meat are decreasing. Tourism offers alternative work. Tourists pay to stay with Sami people in turf huts or Sami tents, take dog-sled or snowmobile rides across the tundra, and sample the life of a herder with reindeers in their natural habitat.

Women and work

Tourism also benefits Sami women. Families used to herd reindeer together, but with the increasing use of large motorised vehicles, men tend to do the herding work, while families stay at home. Many Sami women now work in the tourism industry (for example, selling crafts) and as well as providing them with a higher income, this work preserves Sami culture by enabling the women to continue living in the Sápmi countryside, rather than going to towns to find employment.

▽ Some tourists experience real Sami culture by staying in a Sami tent in the countryside. Traditional Sami tents were once made from reindeer skins, but many are made from waterproof fabric today.

Conserving culture

When tourists experience Sami cultural events, museums or the Sami way of life, they learn about the Sami people and their heritage and this often increases their respect for it and their desire to see it preserved. And far from being tourist attractions, many Sami museums were built to preserve Sami culture first and became tourist attractions later, for example the Siida Museum in Finland which works with young Sami people to document their lives.

In some cases, tourism actually helps preserve some aspects of Sami culture. Tourists are now the main market for Sami handicrafts and without them many of those handicrafts would probably not be produced. As a result of increased demand, some younger people are now learning traditional skills, such as how to make handicrafts and reindeer herding, because now it is possible to earn a living using these skills. To protect themselves against fakes, Sami craftspeople mark their handicrafts with a special seal so that tourists can support local professionals and be certain they are buying genuine Sami handicrafts.

▷ A Sami reindeer herder, one of about 7,000 still working in Finland, tends to his animals in the Arctic town of Rovaniemi.

Community-led tourism

The Sami people of arctic Russia have been gradually forced off much of their tundra grazing-land to make way for oil and gas, minerals and forestry industries. Most live in a town called Lovozero and only a small proportion still herd reindeer. Tourism may prove to be an important industry of the future for the region and its people, if they learn from other examples of Sami tourism. Most successful cultural tourism happens when local communities control it themselves and develop local and cultural resources slowly and thoughtfully.

EXPLORE FURTHER

Find out about Naxi cultural tourism in Lijiang, China, where the World Culture Tourism Forum was held in 2010.

Development or Destruction?

Development

* Cultural tourism provides some Sami people with job opportunities and higher incomes.
* It provides Sami women with work and enables families to stay in the Sápmi countryside.
* It creates a market for traditional Sami handicrafts.
* It increases tourists' understanding and respect for the Sami cultural heritage.

Destruction

* Driving tourists into the Sápmi wilderness can harm the fragile Arctic environment.
* Fake handicrafts and staged Sami cultural events reduce Sami heritage to stereotypes and a commodity.
* Mixing with other cultures can weaken Sami cultural identity.
* Some tourist companies exploit and degrade Sami culture, for example by representing them as 'Santa's helpers'.

Ayia Napa package holidays, Cyprus

Cyprus, off the southern coast of Turkey, is the third largest island in the Mediterranean. It is home to about 1 million people but attracts around 3 million tourists each year who mostly come to enjoy its beaches and Mediterranean climate and long, hot and dry summers.

Ayia Napa resort

In 1974, Ayia Napa on the southern coast of Cyprus was a small fishing village with a population of less than 100 people. Now the entire town is given over to package tourists. The majority of tourists here are 18–30 year olds on package tours. The centre of Ayia Napa is full of clubs and bars that compete with each other to attract tourists using gimmicks such as spraying crowds with popcorn or artificial snow.

Mediterranean Sea

CYPRUS

• Ayia Napa

Mediterranean Sea

Destruction fact

Many locals have moved to a town on a hill nearby to escape from the clubbing culture in the centre of Ayia Napa.

At night, Ayia Napa's main square is filled with tourists visiting the resort's clubs and bars.

Chapter 5

The area has a huge water park and a variety of sports on the beach, such as being pulled through the air on a parachute attached to a speedboat. Albums have been released with Ayia Napa in the title, often based on music played by DJs in the resort.

Cyprus tourism and development

In 1974 the island of Cyprus was partitioned, with Turkey occupying the northern third of the country that included a major port and airport, and Greece occupying the two-thirds in the south. When the GDP of the Greek-Cypriot sector dropped by about one-third by 1975, the Greek government decided tourism was the key to economic growth and set up the Cyprus Tourism Organization to build and control the tourist industry. It worked. Between 1975 and 1983 the average annual rate of growth was about 10 per cent. Tourism became a significant employer both directly, for example in hotels and restaurants, and indirectly, for example construction workers building new hotels. It accounts for 25 to 30 per cent of jobs.

As a result of tourism, Greek Cypriots enjoy a low unemployment rate and a high standard of living and they are among the most prosperous people in the Mediterranean region. The standard of indicators such as infrastructure, services and education is as high as other MEDCs in Europe.

The boom in tourism in Cyprus has also led to a boom in construction on the island.

Development fact

According to the World Travel and Tourism Council, the tourism sector in Cyprus is generating 21.4% of the country's annual GDP and providing a job for 27.2% of those in employment.

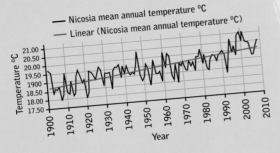

Temperature °C

— Nicosia mean annual temperature °C
— Linear (Nicosia mean annual temperature °C)

21.00
20.50
20.00
19.50
1900
18.50
18.00
17.50

1900 1910 1920 1930 1940 1950 1960 1970 1980 1990 2000 2010

Year

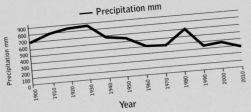

— Precipitation mm

Precipitation mm

900
800
700
600
500
400
300
200
100
0

1900 1910 1920 1930 1940 1950 1960 1970 1980 1990 2000 2010

Year

Water shortages

These charts show the mean annual temperature and precipitation for Nicosia, capital of Cyprus, between 1901 and 2008. As you can see from the charts, as the temperature is gradually increasing, especially in recent years, rainfall is decreasing. In fact, rainfall in Cyprus has dropped by 15 per cent since the 1970s and many experts believe it will drop a further 20 per cent by 2050.

As temperatures increase, water demands increase too but with less rainfall there will be even less to go around and that is why Cyprus is predicted to become the first part of the European Union to run out of water.

A natural resource under threat

The boom in tourism has resulted in higher water use because tourists use more water than locals per capita. Not only do tourists use water for food, drink and hygiene, but leisure facilities such as swimming pools and water parks significantly increase water use. Also, as residents become wealthier from tourism they buy more water-hungry appliances, like washing machines. Cyprus has reached 'peak water', the point at which a country's demand for water outstrips supply. Most of the island's water came from underground aquifers, but groundwater supplies have been emptied. At the coast many aquifers have been so depleted that seawater seeps into the empty spaces making the freshwater salty, so it can't be used for drinking water.

The dry bed of the Kouris Dam near Ayia Napa is evidence of the chronic water shortage in Cyprus.

Water solutions

The situation hit crisis point in 2004–2008 when reservoirs became virtually empty during a drought and the government had to import tankers of fresh water from Greece. Households were rationed and taps only worked for a few hours a day. Now, almost all the drinking water in Greek-Cypriot cities comes from seawater that has had its salt removed in desalination plants. Such plants are expensive to run and energy-intensive so they produce a lot of greenhouse gases, and nor do they replace water in the land. In some areas half of the trees have died because of a lack of water and when trees are lost soil quality drops and this can lead to desertification, the gradual degradation of fertile land into desert.

Water from a wastewater plant in Ayia Napa is used to irrigate fields and hotel gardens in the area.

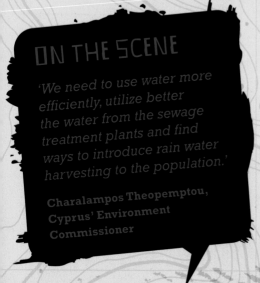

ON THE SCENE

'We need to use water more efficiently, utilize better the water from the sewage treatment plants and find ways to introduce rain water harvesting to the population.'

Charalampos Theopemptou,
Cyprus' Environment
Commissioner

An undersea pipeline is being installed beneath the Mediterranean to carry 75 million cubic meters (2,649 million cubic feet) of drinking water a year from a dam on the Turkish mainland to the northern part of Cyprus. Other government measures include wastewater recycling, in which waste water is filtered and re-used. The water authorities also use measures such as metering of water consumption, water charges, improved farm irrigation systems, and laws restricting the use of hosepipes for car-washing.

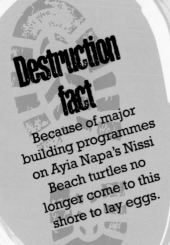

Destruction fact

Because of major building programmes on Ayia Napa's Nissi Beach turtles no longer come to this shore to lay eggs.

Tourists and turtles

Green and loggerhead turtles are under threat, in part due to unintentional killing on fishing hooks and in nets but also as a result of tourist development in Cyprus. On summer nights, female turtles return to beaches on which they hatched to lay their eggs. If disturbed by people, or unable to find a suitable nest site because a beach has been developed, they dump their eggs at sea. In Cyprus, there are now beaches set aside for turtle breeding grounds. When fishing communities make money taking controlled numbers of tourists to see the turtles, they also change their fishing practices. This helps to reduce the number of turtles killed at sea.

Culture shock

In Ayia Napa, tourists' use of drugs and alcohol and subsequent bad behaviour has caused conflict with local communities. For example, in 2008 nine British soldiers were arrested over a bar rampage in Ayia Napa. The 2010 British government report 'British Behaviour Abroad' revealed that Cyprus was the second most likely place for British people to be arrested for drugs abroad. The Cypriot government is clamping down on noise pollution, drunkenness, drugs and public indecency in a drive to shake off Ayia Napa's reputation for bad behaviour.

△ A zoologist helps a green turtle climb out of its nest on a beach in Cyprus.

▽ Tourism officials in Ayia Napa are aiming to rebrand the resort as a holiday destination of great natural beauty.

EXPLORE FURTHER

Find out what is being done to solve the environmental damage caused by beach resort tourism in Goa, India.

Tourism tactics

Tourism in Cyprus has experienced a decline, with 2011 tourist arrivals hitting a 20-year low. This is bad news for a country with a tourism-dependent economy. To encourage a wider range of visitors, especially in winter outside the summer season, the tourist industry is investing in other attractions and in 2009 a golf course was built at Ayia Napa. In arid areas of the Mediterranean it takes about the same amount of water to keep a single 18-hole golf course green for a year as it does to supply 1000 households. So, the government requires each new golf course to have its own desalination plant or use waste water for irrigation. Golf courses are often criticised for water use, but its use of water is no greater than that of a comparable area of irrigated corn and it yields a better financial return.

Development or Destruction?

Development

* Tourism was the key to economic growth in Cyprus in the latter part of the 20th century.
* Tourism accounts for 25-30 per cent of jobs in Cyprus.
* As a result of tourism, Cyprus has a low unemployment rate and Cypriots enjoy a high standard of living.

Destruction

* Use of water by tourists causes severe water stress.
* Beach developments have reduced breeding grounds for endangered sea turtles.
* The behaviour of some tourists in party resorts like Ayia Napa can cause offence to local people.

On safari in Kenya

In the 1970s Kenya became one of the first LEDCs to develop mass tourism. It was also one of the first African countries to offer safaris to tourists, giving people the chance to drive across wild grasslands spotting elephants, zebra, lions, wildebeest and other rare animals.

More than a million tourists came to Kenya in 2010 and the majority visited one of the country's many parks and game reserves. While Kenya's tourism industry is booming, this is not always good news for wildlife or their habitats and it has not provided economic benefits for most ordinary Kenyans, many of whom live in poverty.

▲ **Kenya's Ministry of Tourism has a target of 2 million international tourists by 2012.**

On safari

Safaris were originally hunting expeditions, which began after Europeans began to settle Africa in the late 19th century. A safari consisted of white hunters and a large team of black workers to carry their guns, equipment and supplies, as well as trackers and skinners. The number of safari hunters increased dramatically after the 1950s when air travel made the hunting grounds more accessible. Soon some species were hunted to, or close to, extinction. Sport hunting was banned in Kenya in 1978 and since then tourists go on safari there to shoot animals with cameras, not guns.

Safari holidays and development

After Kenya gained independence from Great Britain in 1963, it invested in tourism as a means of economic development. Tourism is now Kenya's leading earner of foreign currency. Tourism increases revenues in other industries, such as agriculture. It is also a major source of government revenue, from things like taxes, license fees and entry fees, which helps to pay for schools, hospitals and other types of infrastructure.

Africa's national parks were set up to protect wild countryside and animals. Governments pay for rangers to protect the parks by charging tourists for their visits.

Development fact

Today, Africa's national parks cover around 15 per cent of the continent. Kenya has more than 65 national parks and wildlife reserves.

In July many tourists come to Kenya to witness one of the world's greatest wildlife spectacles – the annual migration of millions of wildebeest.

Destruction fact

A study led by the Zoological Society of London found that populations of large mammals in parks across Africa had fallen 59 per cent, on average, from 1970 to 2005. Parks in West Africa had an average population decline of 85 per cent.

This map shows the location of the Masai Mara reserve in Kenya.

Safari holidays and destruction

Some people argue that the safari industry has been too successful. Kenya's famous Masai Mara reserve, for example, has long been the focus of low-revenue, high-volume tourism. That means large numbers of visitors and increasing numbers of safari lodges dotted across the countryside within the reserve. Forests are cleared for lodges, queues of minibuses often get too close and disturb animals, and a high volume of tourist traffic has damaged roads and grasslands. An increased human population around the unfenced reserve has severely depleted the wildlife population.

People and the parks

Most people who work for safari lodges are better-educated workers from other parts of the country, rather than local tribespeople, many of whom now see wild animals as competitors for the land. To protect their livelihoods, some farmers living around the edge of the unfenced Masai Mara reserve kill wildlife that strays onto their land and damages crops or threatens people and livestock. Some local people have to supplement their livelihoods by killing animals for bush meat, cutting down trees for fuel, or poaching wild animals for ivory and skin.

Some studies claim that 95 per cent of the Masai Mara reserve's giraffes have disappeared.

Masai lands

The Masai people were semi-nomadic herders of cattle and goats who lived alongside the wild animals that roamed their Masai Mara lands. The Masai lost some land to the British colonists, and when wildlife parks were created they were evicted from more land that was traditionally theirs. The development of safari parks reduced their roaming area so much that many have given up their pastoral way of life and moved into permanent settlements on poor-quality farmland along the edges of the Mara.

▽ **Masai herders watch over their cattle in the Masai Mara Game Reserve.**

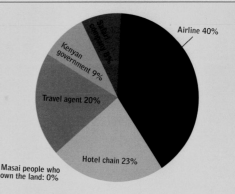

Airline 40%
Kenyan government 9%
Safari company 8%
Travel agent 20%
Hotel chain 23%
Masai people who own the land: 0%

Who profits?

All safari companies and airlines charge different amounts and work in different ways, but this chart shows a breakdown of the economics of an average all-inclusive holiday to Kenya. Most of the profit stays outside Kenya with the airline company, hotel chain and the travel agency. In Kenya levels of corruption are high and corrupt government officials also cream off profits from foreign tourism. Few local people profit at all because most tourist camps employ most of their staff from outside the area. The Masai people, whose lands are used for the safari, usually receive nothing.

37

ON THE SCENE

'The Koiyaki Guiding School has really helped me to understand conservation. We have become the ambassadors for wildlife. I can go and explain to my father, who ... has not understood in the past that we are sitting on a gold mine here in the Mara.'

Dominic Kuluo, a former pupil of the Koiyaki Guiding School

Community benefits

Some tourist companies are selling safari trips to Kenya that conserve the environment and improve the well-being of local people by ensuring that money spent by tourists supports the local community. For example, the Masai Mara eco-lodge, Koiyaki Wilderness Camp, is owned and managed by the local Masai community. The lodges are built from sustainable materials, and local Masai guides take smaller groups of visitors on safaris and the lodges serve meals prepared by local chefs.

A significant proportion of the safari price goes towards supporting community-based Masai Mara conservation and funds the training of safari guides from the local Masai communities at the nearby Koiyaki Guiding School. Students also learn to portray their culture in an interesting and educational way and learn about the local ecosystem and how to manage and help to protect it.

◁ **Betty Maitau, one of the first Masai woman safari guides to graduate from the Koiyaki Guiding School of Kenya.**

EXPLORE FURTHER

Find out about controversial plans for a highway to run through the Serengeti, Tanzania's oldest national park and a UNESCO World Heritage site.

Future impacts?

There are challenges when tourists visit any wild places, as their presence inevitably has an impact. One way to help to protect Kenya's wild places and animals is to ensure that local communities benefit from responsible forms of tourism. In places where tourism provides employment for local people and local communities are direct beneficiaries of income generated by safari camps, local habitats and wildlife become a valuable resource to them too. Whether or not wildlife reserves like the Masai Mara will survive the pressures of increased tourist traffic in future is a matter of debate.

Development or Destruction?

Development

* Tourism accounts for about 10 per cent of Kenya's GDP.
* Tourism aids the development of other Kenyan industries, such as agriculture.
* Tourism is a source of government revenue that helps to pay for infrastructure.
* Tourists help to fund Kenya's national parks, which protect countryside and animals.

Destruction

* Low revenue, high volume tourism impacts on the environment and disturbs wildlife.
* Many Masai tribespeople have moved off their land to make way for national parks.
* Few local people benefit from safari holidays on local land.
* To supplement their livelihoods locals may kill animals for meat, cut down trees for fuel, or poach wild animals.

Sustainable futures

Increasing numbers of holidaymakers are becoming concerned about the destruction tourism can cause, and more people in the tourist industry are trying to create holidays that lessen the negative impact of tourist activities on the environment, natural resources and local communities. This is known as sustainable tourism and it is one of the fastest growing sectors in the tourism industry.

Economic incentives

Tourism can provide huge benefits for local economies, particularly in LEDCs, and supporters of sustainable tourism say it can provide an economic incentive to preserve the environment and increase awareness of unique and fragile ecosystems throughout the world.

For example, unmanaged tourism can damage heritage sites and ecologically sensitive areas, like rainforests, especially famous ones where thousands of tourists want to visit or even climb upon them. If the sites are damaged, tourists will stop coming to see them. Using sustainable practices, tour operators can help to preserve the forests or monuments – and their income for the future – by limiting the numbers of tourists, controlling where they walk and by ensuring that some tourist funds pay to keep the sites in good repair.

△ **It is in tour operators' best interests to help to preserve sites popular with tourists because if the sites are damaged tourists will no longer pay to visit them.**

Development fact

The World Travel and Tourism Council predicts that by 2018, tourism will be worth 80 per cent of the GDP of Antigua and Barbuda, with 95 per cent of all jobs on the two islands related in some way to tourism.

40

Chapter 7

Ecotourism resorts

In some places, sustainable tourism takes the form of purpose-built eco-resorts. The best ecotourism resorts use solar power to heat their water and solar, wind or hydro power to supply their electricity, to reduce emissions from power plants and to avoid running cables to isolated areas. Some compost kitchen and garden waste, and use that compost to grow their own organic food. They minimise water consumption, for example by using greywater for crop irrigation and fitting dry toilets that turn human waste into more compost. Some resorts reduce waste by avoiding buying packaged goods, by recycling and by using biodegradable products. They support local communities by shopping locally and by employing local people, for example as guides or chefs.

The problem with ecotourism projects like this is that it is not always easy for tourists to know which are genuine and which only claim to be offering a sustainable alternative. One way is to look out for accreditation schemes, such as Australia's Ecotourism Certification programme, which list authentic companies and resorts.

Innovations

Some eco-lodges also use vehicles that run on used vegetable oil as well as diesel fuel. These vehicles can run on oil previously used for cooking and can reduce harmful exhaust emissions by over 90 per cent!

▽ **Rainforest villas, or eco-lodges, in Daintree, Queensland, Australia.**

Travel troubles

Some people say that international tourism can never be sustainable, because vehicles such as planes emit polluting gases like carbon dioxide, one of the greenhouse gases experts say cause climate change. The graph on page 7 shows that air passenger numbers are set to increase in future, so what is being done?

Some people try to mitigate the impact of flight emissions with carbon offsetting. This is when people buy carbon offsets, or credits, equal in amount to the carbon dioxide emitted as a result of their trip. These are used to pay for 'green' projects that reduce carbon emissions such as hydropower plants or tree-planting. However, critics of offsetting say it does not deal directly with the immediate pollution caused by travel and takes responsibility away from airlines to do anything to reduce emissions. Some people believe that rises in oil prices will increase the cost and therefore cut the amount of air travel.

Some people choose alternative modes of transport. For example, trains in France run on electricity from nuclear power stations so they are less polluting than oil-fuelled planes.

What can individuals do?

Some people take holidays in their own country to reduce their transport emissions, or they travel by train to a country nearby. Some tourists reduce their emissions by taking fewer long-haul flights, travelling long-distance only every three or four years, for example. Taking fewer holidays for longer also has a positive impact: the daily carbon footprint of a student traveller is just 9 per cent of a business traveller's because the student stays longer in one destination and uses local public transport.

When tourists stay and eat with local families, they learn more about the culture of the place they are visiting and the family gains direct economic benefits.

Can sustainable tourism work?

Some people question whether there can ever be sustainable tourism. There are so many different industries involved in every trip, such as transport firms, hotels, tour operators and restaurants, and it is difficult to make sure that every link in the chain is sustainable. There is also the danger that as sustainable tourism becomes more successful, it will attract big businesses, which could mean more tourists and more destruction.

ON THE SCENE

'We need to find a middle path. We just have to find better ways of taking our holidays - not going to Dubai for three days or New York for shopping when the pound is strong against the dollar.'

Tricia Barnett, director of Tourism Concern

Debate club

Organise a debate to discuss the building of a new island tourist resort. You'll need six people to act as the characters below. They can use information from the book and the statements below to get started.

Each person should be given a chance to speak, without interruptions. Others in the class or group can listen to the speakers in the debate as if they are advisers to the tourism minister. They have to decide whose arguments are most convincing and how and if they will proceed with the project.

PROJECT MANAGER

'I work for a global company with extensive experience in ecotourism. We can ensure tourism benefits us and the people here and that environmental impacts are kept to a minimum.'

WILDLIFE EXPERT

'This region is home to many rare species and building hotels – even eco-lodges – here will affect the wildlife and change this beautiful ecosystem forever.'

FARMER

'We already suffer water shortages. If tourists come, there will be less water for irrigation and local people will have to pay more for their food.'

FISHERMAN

'Because of overfishing, fish stocks are low. If more tourists come I will be able to take them on boat trips and earn a proper living again.'

MOTHER

'A tourist industry would improve the ferry service between our island and the mainland so my children would be able to study in the schools and colleges there.'

VILLAGE LEADER

'If many more tourists come here our way of life will change and our young people will change too. Then no one will remember who the people who lived here really were.'

Glossary

aquifer underground layer of rock that is saturated with water

biodegradable describes something that can decompose or rot easily and safely

carbon footprint direct effect of someone's actions and lifestyle on the environment in terms of carbon dioxide emissions

causeway a road stretching across water

climate change changes in the world's weather patterns caused by human activity

coral reef rock-like structure built by small ocean animals

cultural tourism tourism for those who want to experience the way of life of local people

desalination process that converts salt water into fresh water

displace to force people to move away from their home to another place

dry toilet toilet needing no water for flushing

eco-lodge tourist building that is constructed, run and maintained in sustainable ways

ecotourism form of tourism that strives to minimize ecological impact or damage

emissions substances sent out into the air

erosion gradual wearing away of the earth's surface by water or wind

eutrophication process in which a body of water is enriched by nutrients that cause excessive plant growth and oxygen depletion

GDP abbreviation for Gross Domestic Product – the total value of goods and services produced by a country in one year

globalisation process whereby the world's people are more interconnected and interdependent, linked through technology, etc

GNP abbreviation for Gross National Product, – the value of all goods and services produced within a nation in a given year

greenhouse gas gas in the upper atmosphere that traps the sun's heat

greywater waste water used to flush toilets or for irrigation

groundwater water found below ground

honeypot site popular visitor attraction that attracts large numbers of tourists

indigenous people original inhabitants of an area and their descendants

infrastructure facilities such as roads and water and sewer systems

irrigation supplying water for crops and plants

LEDC less economically developed country

mangrove tropical evergreen trees or shrubs that grow in shallow coastal water

mass tourism traditional, large-scale tourism, such as package holidays

MEDC more economically developed country

multinational describes a group or company that involves or operates in several countries

multiplier effect the 'snowballing' of economic activity, for example increased tourism brings new hotel jobs, and those hotel workers have more money to spend in shops

nutrient substance taken in by plants and animals to help them grow

package holiday a holiday arranged by a travel agent that includes transport, food, lodging and often entertainment or excursions in one price

partitioned describes a country divided by boundaries or borders into different areas owned or run by different people

pastoral describes lifestyle of shepherds who move with livestock to find water and pasture

photosynthesize what plants do to convert carbon dioxide and water into food

poaching taking an animal illegally

semi-nomadic someone who spends part of the year moving from place to place

sustainable using natural resources to meet the needs of the present without jeopardising those resources for future generations

tax money paid to a government

United Nations organization promoting peace, security and economic development

yeti a mysterious, giant ape-like creature

45

Index